Exploring The BUILDING BLOCKS of Science

Book 1

LABORATORY NOTEBOOK

REBECCA W. KELLER, PhD

REAL SCIENCE 4 Kids

Illustrations: Janet Moneymaker

Exploring the Building Blocks of Science Book 1 Laboratory Notebook
ISBN 978-1-936114-31-3

Published by Gravitas Publications Inc.
www.gravitaspublications.com

Contents

Experiment 1

Doing Science

Introduction

In science it is important to do experiments and to write everything down. A laboratory notebook is the place where scientists record what they think, what they observe, and what they discover. Simply put, a laboratory notebook is the place where scientists write down **everything they DO**! This *Laboratory Notebook* will be used for all the *Exploring the Building Blocks of Science: Book 1* experiments. It is the place where you can write down what you learn. Then you will have all the information in one place and can refer to it later.

Each experiment in the *Laboratory Notebook* has five sections. In this first experiment, you will practice using each of the five sections.

I. Think About It

The first section is called *Think About It*. In this section before you do the experiment, you will write down what you think will happen. Thinking about the experiment and what you think you might observe is an important first step in doing science.

Practice using the *Think About It* section. Think about the night sky. Think about what you might see if you were to observe the night sky. On the next page write or draw what you think you might see.

What I Might See in the Night Sky

_____

_____

_____

_____

_____

_____

_____

II. Observe It

The second section is called *Observe It*. In this section you will write down what you observe while you are doing an experiment. It is important to write down exactly what you observe and not what you think you should observe.

Practice using the *Observe It* section. Pick an evening to observe the night sky. Make an observation by looking at as many details as possible.

Some details to observe:

- Are there clouds in the sky?

- Can you see the Moon?

- How many stars can you see in the sky?

- Can you tell if the stars have any color?

- What else can you observe?

In the following space write or draw what you actually observe.

(Note: In some experiments the *Observe It* section will come first and the *Think About It* section will be second.)

Observations of the Night Sky

_____

_____

_____

_____

_____

_____

_____

_____

III. What Did You Discover?

The third section is called *What Did You Discover?* This section will have several questions for you to answer about what you observed. Don't worry about whether your answers are right or wrong. There are no right answers for this section. Your answers may be different from what you thought you would observe or from the answers that other students write down.

Practice using the *What Did You Discover?* section by answering the following questions. Refer to the notes you made in the *Observe It* section.

❶ What color was the night sky?

_____

_____

_____

_____

❷ Did you see the Moon? Why or why not?

_____

_____

_____

_____

❸ If you did see the Moon, was it round? Why or why not?

_____

_____

_____

_____

❹ Did you see stars in the sky? Why or why not?

_____

_____

_____

_____

❺ If you did see stars, were they all the same color?

_____

_____

_____

_____

❻ What else did you observe?

_____

_____

_____

_____

IV. Why?

The fourth section is called *Why?*. This section has a brief discussion about what you might have observed.

By looking at the night sky you can observe many different things. If the sky is free of clouds, you might see lots of stars of different sizes and groupings. You might see a bright Moon or no Moon. If you live in a city, the city lights might make it hard to see the stars. If you live in the country, away from city lights, you will likely see lots of stars on a cloudless night. If there are clouds in the sky, you might see only the clouds that are covering the stars and the Moon, or you might see the Moon and some stars in between the clouds.

V. Just For Fun

The last section is called *Just For Fun*. This section has an extra experiment or activity for you to do.

Practice using the *Just For Fun* section by creating your own experiment about making an observation. You can use the following outline for the five sections. Think of an experiment for observing a frog or an ant or a plant.

You will be writing or drawing the instructions for the experiment, and then your parent or teacher will do the experiment by following your instructions. Give each section of your experiment to your parent or teacher as you finish it. Have them do each of the five sections with you, one at a time.

Experiment Title _____

I. Think About It

(What should the person doing this experiment think about before starting the experiment?)

_____

_____

_____

(Have the person doing the experiment write or draw what they think they might see.)

_____

_____

_____

_____

_____

II. Observe It

(What kinds of things should the person doing this experiment look for?)

_____

_____

_____

(Have the person doing the experiment write or draw what they actually observe.)

_____

_____

_____

_____

_____

III. What Did You Discover?

(Think of some questions can you ask about what was observed, and then have the person doing the experiment answer them.)

❶ _____

_____

_____

_____

❷ _____

_____

_____

_____

❸ _____

_____

_____

_____

❹ _____

_____

_____

_____

IV. Why?

(Write or draw why you think the person doing the experiment observed the things they did.)

_____

_____

_____

_____

_____

_____

V. Just For Fun

(Make up an extra activity to go along with your experiment. Write or draw instructions for this section.

_____

_____

_____

_____

_____

_____

(Have the person doing the experiment follow your instructions and write about or draw your *Just For Fun* activity. Or you can do this activity yourself.)

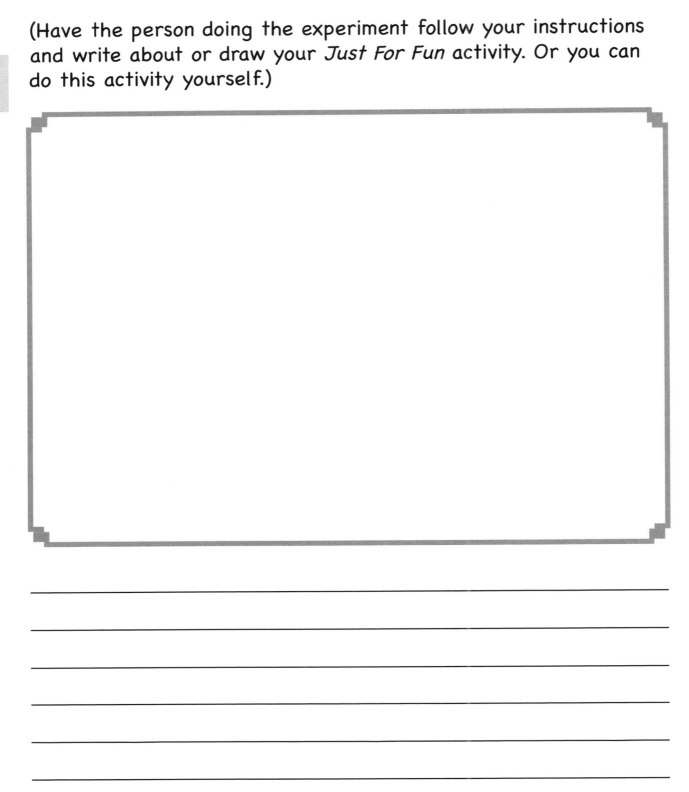

_____

_____

_____

_____

_____

_____

Experiment 2

Chemistry Every Day

People have always used chemistry in their lives, but before it became a science, people did not know how chemistry made things work. In this experiment you will explore how you use chemistry every day.

I. Think About It

❶ Think about whether or not the things you do in a day involve any chemistry. Think about what you do, where you go, and what you eat.

❷ Make a list of some of the things you do in a day.

_____

_____

_____

_____

_____

_____

❸ Do any of these activities involve chemistry? Why or why not?

_____

_____

_____

_____

_____

_____

II. Observe It

Make a list of everything you do in one day. Start with the first thing you do in the morning and observe yourself throughout the day. Write down what you do, what you eat, how your food is prepared, where you go, and how you get there.

CHEMISTRY

_____

_____

_____

_____

_____

_____

_____

_____

_____

_____

_____

_____

_____

_____

_____

CHEMISTRY

III. What Did You Discover?

❶ Do you use chemistry when you brush your teeth with toothpaste? Why or why not?

_____

_____

_____

❷ Do you use chemistry when cooking food? Why or why not?

_____

_____

_____

❸ Do you use chemistry when you eat food? Why or why not?

_____

_____

_____

❹ Do you use chemistry when you ride in a car? Why or why not?

_____

_____

_____

CHEMISTRY

IV. Why?

Chemistry is the study of physical things and the matter things are made of. Chemists are scientists who do experiments to find out what physical things are like and how they change. Sometimes when matter is heated or when different kinds of matter are mixed together, a chemical process will make a change take place. By doing experiments, chemists can discover useful changes that happen to physical things. For example, chemists discovered which things when mixed together will make a soap that will take stains out of clothes.

Many daily activities use chemistry. Toothpaste is made of chemicals that help keep your teeth clean and your gums healthy. Cooking changes the chemistry of food. Eggs solidify with heat because of chemistry. Your body uses chemistry to digest the food you eat. A car is powered by the chemistry of gasoline. Painting a picture involves making mixtures and using chemicals that give off particular colors. All of these activities use chemistry.

V. Just For Fun

Use watercolor paints for this part of the experiment.

❶ Mix blue and red together. What color do you get?

_____

❷ Mix blue and yellow together. What color do you get?

_____

❸ Mix yellow and red together. What color do you get?

_____

❹ How many colors do you need to mix together to make black?

_____

❺ Experiment with mixing the paint in different color combinations and see how many colors you can make.

❻ When the paint is dry, cut out some examples of your mixtures and tape them on the next page.

CHEMISTRY

CHEMISTRY

Paint Mixtures

What Is It Made Of?

I. Think About It

Write down the name of an object. Using words and drawings, describe any features you think it has.

_____   _____   _____   _____

_____   _____   _____   _____

_____   _____   _____   _____

II. Observe It

Write down the name of the object you thought about. Describe what you actually see, using words and drawings.

_____   _____   _____   _____
_____   _____   _____   _____
_____   _____   _____   _____

I. Think About It

Write down the name of an object. Using words and drawings, describe any features you think it has.

_____   _____   _____   _____

_____   _____   _____   _____

_____   _____   _____   _____

II. Observe It

Write down the name of the object you thought about. Describe what you actually see, using words and drawings.

_____   _____   _____   _____
_____   _____   _____   _____
_____   _____   _____   _____

I. Think About It

Write down the name of an object. Using words and drawings, describe any features you think it has.

CHEMISTRY

_____   _____   _____   _____

_____   _____   _____   _____

_____   _____   _____   _____

II. Observe It

Write down the name of the object you thought about. Describe what you actually see, using words and drawings.

_____   _____   _____   _____

_____   _____   _____   _____

_____   _____   _____   _____

I. Think About It

Write down the name of an object. Using words and drawings, describe any features you think it has.

_____   _____   _____   _____
_____   _____   _____   _____
_____   _____   _____   _____

II. Observe It

Write down the name of the object you thought about. Describe what you actually see, using words and drawings.

_____   _____   _____   _____
_____   _____   _____   _____
_____   _____   _____   _____

III. What Did You Discover?

❶ Were the objects you looked at the same as you expected them to be or were they different?

_____

_____

❷ How were they the same as you expected?

_____

_____

❸ How were they different from what you expected?

_____

_____

❹ Did you expect the objects to be the same on the inside and the outside or to be different?

_____

_____

❺ Which ones were the same on the inside and the outside?

_____

_____

❻ Which ones were different on the inside and the outside?

_____

_____

IV. Why?

When we look at things around us, we often don't notice the small details. In fact, some things are too small to see with our eyes. Atoms, for example, are too small to see with our eyes, but by doing experiments scientists have discovered that everything is made of atoms.

When we take the time to look for small details, we often find amazing things we have never seen before. For example, we notice that some of the things we see are similar to each other. Different kinds of crackers, for instance, have some things that are the same as each other. Many crackers are square or round and the crackers in one box are often the same shape.

However, we also notice that even though two things may seem the same, they are not exactly the same. No two round crackers are exactly the same, and no two square crackers are exactly the same. Each one is unique. We can see the ways in which things are unique when we look at the little details.

The same is true of you. You may look similar to your mom or dad, sister or brother, but you are not exactly the same. You, too, are unique.

CHEMISTRY

V. Just For Fun

Think of a family member or friend. What things can you observe that are similar about you and the other person? What things are different?

List or draw things that are similar.

CHEMISTRY

_____

_____

_____

_____

_____

_____

_____

_____

_____

_____

_____

_____

_____

_____

List or draw things that are different.

Follow the Rules!

I. Think About It

You are going to make "molecules" with toothpicks and marshmallows. First, think about what you might find out.

❶ If you could use as many toothpicks and as many marshmallows as you wanted to, how many different shapes do you think you could make?

_____

❷ If you could stick only three toothpicks into a big marshmallow, how many shapes do you think you could make?

_____

❸ If you could stick only two toothpicks into a big marshmallow, how many shapes do you think you could make?

_____

❹ If you could stick only one toothpick into a big marshmallow, how many shapes do you think you could make?

_____

❺ What if you could not use any toothpicks at all? Could you make any shapes? Why or why not?

_____

_____

_____

_____

CHEMISTRY

II. Observe It

❶ Make as many different "molecules" as you can with the marshmallows and toothpicks.

How many can you make? _____

Can you draw one?

❷ This time you can put only three toothpicks into a big marshmallow. Following this rule, make as many different molecules as you can. A small marshmallow will go on the other end of each toothpick.

How many can you make? _____

Can you draw one?

❸ Now you can put only two toothpicks into a big marshmallow. Following this rule, make as many different molecules as you can. A small marshmallow will go on the other end of each toothpick.

How many can you make? _____

Can you draw one?

❹ Now you can put only one toothpick into a big marshmallow. Following this rule, make as many different molecules as you can. A small marshmallow will go on the other end of the toothpick.

How many can you make? _____

Can you draw one?

❺ Compare the molecules you made when you had rules to follow with the molecules you made when you did not have rules to follow.

Which ones are the same?

Can you draw two that are the same?

❻ Again compare the molecules you made when you had rules to follow with the molecules you made when you did not have rules to follow.

Which ones are different?

Can you draw two that are different?

CHEMISTRY

III. What Did You Discover?

CHEMISTRY

❶ How many molecules could you make without using any rules?

_____

❷ How many molecules could you make with the rules?

_____

❸ When using the "rules," could you make more molecules or fewer molecules than without the rules?

_____

❹ Why could you make more (or fewer)?

_____

_____

_____

_____

_____

_____

_____

IV. Why?

Atoms cannot make molecules any way they want to. When atoms come together to make molecules, they must follow rules. Because they follow rules, only a certain number of molecules can be formed.

Why do you think there are rules that atoms follow when making molecules? What do you think would happen if atoms could form any kind of molecule?

Why do you have to follow rules? What do you think would happen if you could do anything you wanted to? What do you think would happen if anyone could do anything they wanted to and there were no rules at all?

Think for a moment what kind of world it might be without any rules. Chances are it would be a very difficult world to live in. Rules bring order to our lives. For the same reason, rules are important when molecules are being formed—they bring order to the process. Rules help make all of the things in the world "ordered."

V. Just For Fun

Think of a game that you like to play and list all the rules you can think of for that game. Why are these rules important when you play the game?

OR

Make up your own game and make up the rules that would be needed to play it. What name would you give your new game?

Game's Name _____

Rules _____

_____

_____

_____

_____

_____

_____

_____

_____

_____

_____

_____

_____

_____

What Will Happen?

CHEMISTRY

I. Think About It

Look at all of the things on the table. Describe them.

What do they smell like?

A _____

B _____

C _____

D _____

What color are they?

A _____

B _____

C _____

D _____

Are they thick or thin?

A _____

B _____

C _____

D _____

II. Observe It

❶ What will happen if you add **A** to **B**?
Can you guess?

_____

_____

Now, add **A** to **B**.
What happened?
Describe what happened and draw a picture.

_____

_____

_____

CHEMISTRY

❷ What will happen if you add **A** to **C**?
Can you guess?

_____

_____

Now, add **A** to **C**.
What happened?
Describe what happened and draw a picture.

_____

_____

_____

_____

_____

❸ What will happen if you add **A** to **D**?
   Can you guess?

_____

_____

Now, add **A** to **D**.
What happened?
Describe what happened and draw a picture.

_____

_____

_____

_____

CHEMISTRY

❹ **What will happen if you add B to C?**
Can you guess?

_____

_____

Now, add B to C.
What happened?
Describe what happened and draw a picture.

_____

_____

_____

_____

❺ What will happen if you add **B** to **D**?
Can you guess?

_____

_____

Now, add **B** to **D**.
What happened?
Describe what happened and draw a picture.

_____

_____

_____

_____

_____

❻ **What will happen if you add C to D?**
Can you guess?

_____

_____

Now, add C to D.
What happened?
Describe what happened and draw a picture.

_____

_____

_____

_____

Summary

Summarize your answers.

❶ Did lemon juice (**A**) react with vinegar (**B**)? _____

❷ Did lemon juice (**A**) react with milk (**C**)? _____

❸ Did lemon juice (**A**) react with baking soda (**D**)? _____

❹ Did vinegar (**B**) react with milk (**C**)? _____

❺ Did vinegar (**B**) react with baking soda (**D**)? _____

❻ Did milk (**C**) react with baking soda (**D**)? _____

❼ What things did you notice that told you whether a reaction took place or did not take place?

_____

_____

_____

_____

_____

_____

CHEMISTRY

CHEMISTRY

III. What Did You Discover?

❶ What happened when you added **A** to **B**?

_____

❷ What happened when you added **A** to **D**?

_____

❸ Were they different? If so, how?

_____

❹ Were some of the reactions the same? Which ones?

_____

❺ Could you guess what would happen before you added them together?

_____

❻ Did you guess correctly?

_____

❼ Why or why not?

_____

_____

_____

_____

_____

IV. Why?

Why did some of the liquids you mixed react and some did not? It turns out that not every molecule will react with every other molecule. Molecules follow "rules" when they react, just like atoms follow rules to make molecules. The rules tell the molecules which molecules they can react with and which molecules they can't react with.

Vinegar and lemon juice both react with milk. Vinegar and lemon juice also both react with baking soda. Vinegar and lemon juice are similar to each other. That is why they react in similar ways.

Although both vinegar and lemon juice reacted with milk and baking soda, the reactions were different. When added to milk, the vinegar and the lemon juice each made the milk curdle. When added to baking soda, the vinegar and the lemon juice each made bubbles. Milk and baking soda do not have the same type of molecules in them, so they had different types of chemical reactions with the vinegar and the lemon juice. The molecules combined in different ways.

V. Just For Fun

Try another mixing experiment to see what will happen.

Put some baking soda in a cup. Add some sugar. Now pour in some vinegar. What happens? Is it different from what happened when you mixed just baking soda and vinegar without the sugar? On the next page, write or draw what you observe.

If you like, you can repeat this experiment, using differing amounts of baking soda, sugar, and vinegar. Observe whether this makes a difference in the reaction.

CHEMISTRY

Or, find two food items in your kitchen that you haven't already used in a mixture. What do you think might happen when you mix them together? Now mix them. What actually happens? Write or draw what you observe. You can repeat this experiment by mixing the two items in different amounts, or you can try mixing other combinations of two food items.

Experiment 6

What Is Life?

I. Think About It

Biology is the study of life. In this experiment you will explore the differences between living things and non-living things.

❶ What do you think the differences are between life and non-life?

_____

_____

_____

_____

_____

_____

_____

_____

❷ What do you think makes you different from a rock?

_____

_____

_____

_____

_____

_____

_____

_____

BIOLOGY

❸ What do you think makes a frog different from a table?

_____

_____

_____

_____

_____

_____

_____

❹ Do you think a rock ever dies? Why or why not?

_____

_____

_____

_____

_____

_____

_____

_____

BIOLOGY

II. Observe It

Find one living thing and one non-living thing to observe. Write the name of each thing in the space provided on the next page. Use the following questions to help with your observations.

- Can the item move?

- Does the item breathe?

- Does the item consume food?

- Can the item reproduce itself?

- What else can you notice?

Write or draw your observations in the spaces on the next page.

Living Thing	Non-Living Thing
_____	_____

Write

_____	_____
_____	_____
_____	_____
_____	_____
_____	_____
_____	_____
_____	_____
_____	_____

Living Thing	Non-Living Thing
_____	_____

Draw

BIOLOGY

III. What Did You Discover?

❶ List four things that are different between living things and non-living things.

_____

_____

_____

_____

_____

❷ If you traveled to a faraway planet, how would you know which things were alive and which were not alive?

_____

_____

_____

_____

_____

❸ Write your own definition of life.

_____

_____

_____

_____

_____

BIOLOGY

IV. Why?

Biology is the study of life. The first step in studying life is knowing what is alive and what is not alive. It can be very easy to know the difference between something that is alive and something that is not alive. However, defining life can be challenging, even for scientists. In general, living things consume some sort of food source, reproduce themselves, and respond to their environment.

V. Just For Fun

Imagine that you have traveled to a faraway planet that no one has ever been to before. Using your imagination, think about the kinds of living things you might discover there. Think of as many details as you can, and then write about or draw pictures of these imagined living things on the faraway planet.

What would you name this planet? Do the imaginary creatures have names? Record your ideas on the next page.

BIOLOGY

Living Things on Planet _____

Experiment 7

Where Does It Go?

I. Observe It

❶ Collect some different objects to observe.

❷ Look carefully at the objects and make observations about them.

❸ In the spaces provided, name each object and describe each in detail using words or pictures.

BIOLOGY

BIOLOGY

BIOLOGY

BIOLOGY

II. Think About It

❶ Look at all of the objects you described. Think about different groups you might use to sort them. You might use small or round or white or fuzzy.

❷ Name five groups you will use to sort the objects. Put the name of each group in the gray box. Put each object in **ONE** group only.

❸ Are there objects that fit in more than one group? If so, re-sort as many objects as you can into new groups.

❹ Can you do it again?

III. What Did You Discover?

❶ What did you observe about the objects you collected?

_____

_____

_____

_____

_____

❷ Was it easy to pick groups to sort the objects? Why or why not?

_____

_____

_____

_____

_____

❸ Was it easy to decide which objects would go in each group? Why or why not?

_____

_____

_____

_____

BIOLOGY

❹ The objects in a group have the same feature (for example, round or small). List some features that were different between objects in the same group.

The _____ objects

were all _____ but some

were also _____ .

The _____ objects

were all _____ but some

were also _____ .

The _____ objects

were all _____ but some

were also _____ .

The _____ objects

were all _____ but some

were also _____ .

The _____ objects

were all _____ but some

were also _____ .

IV. Why?

It can be hard to sort objects into groups. Some round objects may also be fuzzy, like a cotton ball. And some other round objects might be smooth like a rubber ball. Some smooth objects might also be large. And some smooth objects might also be small. How do you decide which object to put in which group?

This can be a difficult problem, even for scientists. Living things have lots of different features, and it can be hard to figure out which living things go in which groups. Do you sort all the green creatures in one group and all the brown creatures in another group? This would be one way to sort green grass and bears. But what about a tree? A tree is both green and brown. Does a tree go with the grass or with the bears?

Scientists sometimes discover a new living thing—a creature they have never seen before. The first thing a scientist does is make careful observations about the creature. Is it green or gray? Does it have smooth skin or scaly skin? Does it live in the water, or does it live on land? Does it eat vegetables, or does it eat other animals? Can you see it with your eyes, or do you need to use a microscope to see it?

All of these observations help scientists know which group a new creature should go into. By putting it into a group, scientists can better understand what is the same and what is different about the new creature compared to other creatures.

BIOLOGY

V. Just For Fun

You are an explorer traveling to places on Earth where no one has been before. In one of these remote areas, you find a new creature that no one knows about. It has the following features.

- It is green.

- It eats flies.

- It lives in trees.

- It flies with wings.

If you had to put your new creature into a group, would you group it with frogs, monkeys, or butterflies?

Draw a picture of this new creature.

The scientist who discovers a new living thing gets to name it. What would you name this creature you found?

A New Creature

BIOLOGY

Experiment 8

What Do You Need?

I. Observe It

❶ Cells are like little cities. There are lots of jobs that need to be done by lots of different workers inside a city, and there are lots of jobs that need to be done inside a cell.

Your mom and dad also do lots of different jobs at your house. Observe some jobs that your parent does during the day.

List some jobs that you observe your mom or dad doing at your house.

Job	
Job	
Job	
Job	
Job	
Job	
Job	

❷ Pick one of the jobs you listed, and think about all the tools or items you think your mom or dad would need to have when doing this job.

Write the name of the job and list or draw the items you think would be needed to do the job.

Job	
Items Needed	

❸ Draw a picture showing your mom or dad doing their job with the items needed to do it.

Job _____

❹ Pick one of the items your mom or dad uses to do their job. Draw a picture of the item, showing details.

Item _____

Job _____

II. Think About It

For the item you drew, answer the following questions verbally or in writing.

❶ What is the item?

_____

❷ Where did the item come from?

_____

_____

❸ How did the item get there?

_____

_____

❹ Who made the item?

_____

_____

❺ What is the item made of?

_____

_____

❻ Where does the material that the item is made of come from?

_____

_____

_____

III. What Did You Discover?

❶ Think about all the different jobs that your mom or dad does in your house. Make a list of these jobs.

_____

_____

_____

_____

_____

BIOLOGY

❷ How many items does your mom or dad need to have when doing these jobs? List these items.

_____

_____

_____

_____

_____

❸ How many people does it take to make the item you drew in Step **❹** of *I. Observe It?* List as many as you can.

_____

_____

_____

_____

_____

❹ If your mom or dad had to make their own item to do the job, how many more jobs would they need to do? List a few.

_____

_____

_____

_____

❺ If your mom or dad had to make all of the items in your house, how many jobs do you think they would have? List a few.

_____

_____

_____

_____

❻ Do you think it helps to have a city that can make certain items so your mom and dad can buy the items they need to have in order to do other jobs?

_____

_____

_____

_____

BIOLOGY

IV. Why?

Think about all of the items your mom and dad need to have when doing certain jobs in your house. Notice that they need lots of different items because there are lots of different jobs. It takes lots of different people doing lots of different jobs in different parts of the city or country to make the items your mom or dad uses.

A cell works in much the same way as a city works. There are places in the cell where different jobs get done, and there are lots of different types of molecules that are needed for a cell to do those jobs. In order for a cell to live, a cell must make many of these molecules itself. In a cell, there are many molecules doing many different jobs to make all of the molecules a cell needs.

Each part of a cell has a different job to do. And each job a cell does needs different molecules. A cell must make sure all of the molecules it needs for living are in the right places at the right time and in the right amount.

When a cell does not have all the molecules it needs to do all the jobs it has to do, or when a cell does not have enough molecules, or when the jobs are not done in the right way, the cell cannot live. In a similar way, a city would not work if people were not doing the right jobs, or were not in the right place at the right time, or if the jobs were not done in the right way.

V. Just For Fun

Observe one of the items your mom or dad uses to do a job.

- What materials is it made of?

- How many different materials can you observe?

- Choose one of these materials and look up the way it is made. Write about or draw what you find out.

Job _____

Experiment 9

Yummy Yogurt

I. Think About It

What do you think the differences are between milk and yogurt?
Write your answer below.

_____

_____

_____

_____

_____

_____

_____

_____

_____

_____

_____

_____

_____

_____

_____

BIOLOGY

II. Observe It

In the space below, write down the differences you observe between milk and yogurt.

Milk	Yogurt

BIOLOGY

III. What Did You Discover?

❶ How did the yogurt smell?

_____

_____

_____

❷ Was the yogurt thicker than the milk?

_____

_____

_____

❸ What did the yogurt taste like?

_____

_____

_____

❹ How did the yogurt feel in your hands? Did it feel different from the milk? Why or why not?

_____

_____

_____

_____

IV. Why?

Although yogurt is made from milk, yogurt looks, feels, tastes, and smells different from regular milk.

When bacteria are added to milk, the bacteria produce lactic acid. This causes changes to the milk that turn the milk into yogurt. These changes make yogurt thicker than regular milk and give yogurt a particular smell and taste.

When you eat yogurt that contains "live and active cultures," you are eating live bacteria. The bacteria found in yogurt are bacteria that are good for you. They help you digest the yogurt.

V. Just For Fun

Try making your own yogurt mixtures. What other foods could you add to the yogurt to change its taste or color?

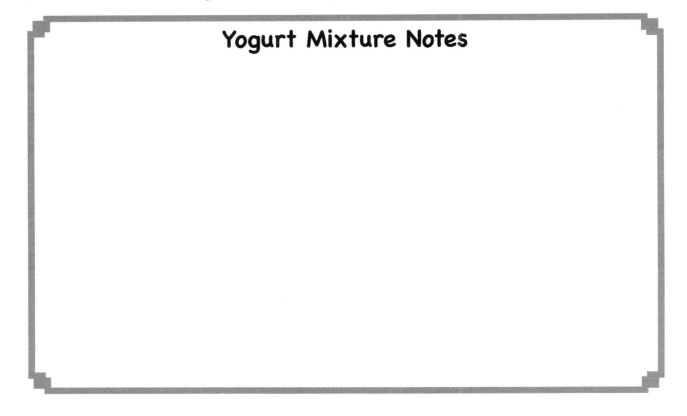

Yogurt Mixture Notes

Experiment 10

Falling Objects

I. Observe It

❶ Take two tennis balls and hold them at chest level with your arms pointing straight out in front of you.

❷ Release the two objects from your hands at the same time.

❸ Watch carefully to see how they land.

❹ In the following box use words or pictures to record what you see.

❺ Repeat Steps ❶-❹ using different objects such as:

- An orange and an apple.
- A tennis ball and a rubber ball.
- An apple and a tennis ball.
- A rubber ball and an apple.
- An orange and a tennis ball.

PHYSICS

Object 1 _____

Object 2 _____

_____

_____

_____

_____

_____

_____

_____

Object 1 _____

Object 2 _____

_____

_____

_____

_____

_____

_____

_____

Object 1 _____

Object 2 _____

_____

_____

_____

_____

_____

_____

_____

Object 1 _____

Object 2 _____

_____

_____

_____

_____

_____

_____

_____

PHYSICS

Object 1 _____

Object 2 _____

_____

_____

_____

_____

_____

_____

_____

PHYSICS

Object 1 _____

Object 2 _____

_____

_____

_____

_____

_____

_____

_____

PHYSICS

Object 1 _____

Object 2 _____

_____

_____

_____

_____

_____

_____

_____

II. Think About It

❶ Did the objects fall at the same speed? How can you tell?

_____

_____

_____

_____

❷ Are there any changes you could make to your experiment?
Holding the objects higher? Holding the objects lower?
Describe changes you can make.

_____

_____

_____

_____

_____

_____

_____

_____

❸ Repeat the experiment for one set of objects using one
change you thought about.

❹ Record your observations on the next page.

PHYSICS

Object 1 _____

Object 2 _____

Change to Experiment _____

_____

_____

_____

_____

_____

_____

_____

_____

III. What Did You Discover?

❶ Was it easy or difficult to release the objects at the same time? Why or why not?

_____

_____

_____

❷ Was it easy or difficult to observe the objects falling? Why or why not?

_____

_____

_____

❸ For each of the pairs of objects, did both objects land at the same time? Why or why not?

_____

_____

_____

❹ Did the changes you chose to make to your experiment make a difference? Why or why not?

_____

_____

_____

_____

_____

PHYSICS

IV. Why?

Galileo Galilei discovered that when he let two objects of different weights fall from the same height, they always landed at the same time. This seems the opposite of what you might think would happen. It seems like a heavier object would fall faster than a lighter object. But this is not what happens. Your observations showed that two objects of different weights will hit the ground at the same time. Why?

Things fall because of gravity. Gravity is a force that makes the objects on Earth stay on Earth. (You will learn about forces in a following chapter.) Gravity pulls everything down towards the center of the Earth. When you hold two objects in your hands, gravity is pulling on them. Every object has gravity pulling on it all the time. Gravity pulls on apples in the same way that it pulls on tennis balls. Gravity pulls on oranges in the same way that it pulls on rubber balls. Everything has the same force of gravity pulling on it at the same time. So an apple (which is heavier than a tennis ball) has the same amount of gravity pulling on it as the tennis ball. Both the tennis ball and the apple start off with exactly the same amount of gravity pulling on them at the same time, and the amount of gravity pulling on them never changes.

Once the objects are released, they fall at the same speed because they have the same amount of gravity pulling on them at the same time. It doesn't matter how heavy they are. That is what Galileo and YOU discovered by doing this experiment.

PHYSICS

V. Just For Fun

What do you think would happen if you dropped an orange and a cotton ball or a feather at the same time?

Try it. Record your observations.

Object 1 _Orange_

Object 2 _Cotton Ball (or Feather)_

PHYSICS

Experiment 11

Get To Work!

I. Observe It

❶ Take a marshmallow and observe its color, shape, and size. Write or draw your observations in the "Before" space on the following page.

❷ Take the marshmallow and place it in the center of your palm.

❸ Close your hand around the marshmallow and squeeze it with your palm and fingers.

❹ Observe your effort—muscles, hands, and fingers.

❺ Observe the marshmallow after you have squeezed it. Write or draw your observations in the space next to "After."

❻ Repeat Steps **❶-❺** with several other objects such as:

- rubber ball

- tennis ball

- lemon or lime

- rock

- banana

PHYSICS

Marshmallow

Before

_____

_____

_____

_____

_____

_____

_____

_____

_____

_____

After

_____

_____

_____

_____

_____

_____

_____

_____

_____

_____

PHYSICS

_____

Before

_____

_____

_____

_____

_____

_____

_____

_____

_____

_____

_____

PHYSICS

After

_____

_____

_____

_____

_____

_____

_____

_____

_____

_____

_____

Before

_____

_____

_____

_____

_____

_____

_____

_____

_____

_____

After

_____

_____

_____

_____

_____

_____

_____

_____

_____

_____

PHYSICS

Before

_____
_____
_____
_____
_____
_____
_____
_____
_____
_____

After

_____
_____
_____
_____
_____
_____
_____
_____
_____
_____

Before

_____

_____

_____

_____

_____

_____

_____

_____

_____

_____

After

_____

_____

_____

_____

_____

_____

_____

_____

_____

_____

PHYSICS

_____

Before

_____

_____

_____

_____

_____

_____

_____

_____

_____

_____

After

_____

_____

_____

_____

_____

_____

_____

_____

_____

_____

PHYSICS

Before

_____

_____

_____

_____

_____

_____

_____

_____

_____

_____

After

_____

_____

_____

_____

_____

_____

_____

_____

_____

_____

PHYSICS

II. Think About It

❶ How did the objects feel in your hands?

_____

_____

_____

_____

_____

❷ Were some objects easier to squeeze in your hand than other objects? Were some objects harder to squeeze in your hand than other objects?

_____

_____

_____

_____

_____

PHYSICS

❸ On the next page, create a summary of your observations. List those objects that were easy to squeeze and those objects that were hard to squeeze.

❹ Put a circle around the object on which you believe your hand did the most work.

❺ Put a rectangle around the object on which you believe your hand did the least work.

Easy to Squeeze

_____

_____

_____

_____

_____

_____

_____

_____

_____

_____

Hard to Squeeze

_____

_____

_____

_____

_____

_____

_____

_____

_____

_____

PHYSICS

III. What Did You Discover?

❶ For the objects that were easy to squeeze, how much force did you need?

_____

_____

❷ For the objects that were hard to squeeze, how much force did you need?

_____

_____

❸ Did you do more or less work on the objects that were easy to squeeze?

_____

_____

❹ Did you do more or less work on the objects that were hard to squeeze?

_____

_____

❺ Was this result what you expected? Why or why not?

_____

_____

_____

_____

_____

PHYSICS

IV. Why?

In this experiment you squeezed several objects between the palm and fingers of your hand. You used your hands like a little force tool. You can do this because your hand has lots of nerve endings that can detect how soft or hard an object is. You can also tell with your body how easy or hard it is to squeeze an object by noticing your muscles and breath. You can tell with your body if more or less force is needed to change the shape of an object. You can also tell with your body if more or less energy is required to generate the force.

Do you do more work if you use more force and more energy? Not necessarily. You may have noticed that you could easily smash the marshmallow, but it was harder to smash the rubber ball, tennis ball, or rock. Depending on your results, you may have used more force to try to change the shape of the tennis ball or rock, but if they did not actually change shape, you didn't end up doing any work!

PHYSICS

V. Just For Fun

First, squeeze a tennis ball with your hand. Then, use a pair of pliers to squeeze the tennis ball. Observe whether the tennis ball changes shape. Also observe whether it is easier or harder to change the shape of the tennis ball with a pair of pliers than with your hand.

Record your observations.

Tennis Ball

Without Pliers	With Pliers

Experiment 12

Moving Energy in a Toy Car

I. Observe It

❶ Take the board or sheet of cardboard and lay it flat on the ground. Place the toy car on the board or cardboard sheet. Without rolling the toy car, observe what happens.

❷ Write or draw your observations in the space below.

Car — flat

_____

_____

_____

_____

_____

_____

_____

_____

_____

_____

_____

_____

_____

_____

_____

_____

PHYSICS

❸ Now, lift the board or cardboard sheet to the height of your ankles, making a ramp. Again observe what happens. Note whether or not the toy car moves. If it does move, note how it moves.

❹ Write or draw your observations in the space below.

Car lifted to ankles

❺ Now lift the ramp to the height of your knees. Again observe what happens. Note whether or not the toy car moves. If it does move, note how it moves.

❻ Write or draw your observations in the space provided below.

Car lifted to knees

_____

_____

_____

_____

_____

_____

_____

_____

_____

_____

_____

_____

_____

_____

PHYSICS

❼ Now lift the ramp to the height of your hips. Again observe what happens. Note whether or not the toy car moves. If it does move, note how it moves.

❽ Write or draw your observations in the space provided below.

Car lifted to hips

❾ Now lift the ramp to the height of your chest. Again observe what happens. Note whether or not the toy car moves. If it does move, note how it moves.

❿ Write or draw your observations in the space provided below.

Car lifted to chest

PHYSICS

Collect Your Results

In the space below create a table showing your results.

Height of Car	Observations
Car flat	
Car lifted to ankles	
Car lifted to knees	
Car lifted to hips	
Car lifted to chest	

II. Think About It

❶ Think about what the toy car did as you lifted the ramp higher and higher.

❷ Review what you learned in your *Student Textbook* about gravitational stored energy. Recall that gravitational stored energy exists in objects that are elevated above the ground.

❸ Think about both the toy car and gravitational stored energy. Guess which car height had the least amount of gravitational stored energy and which car height had the greatest amount of gravitational stored energy. Record your answers.

Least _____

Most _____

❹ In the chart on the following page, put a circle around the car that had the least amount of gravitational stored energy.

❺ Put a rectangle around the car that had the greatest amount of gravitational stored energy.

PHYSICS

Car flat

Car lifted to ankles

Car lifted to knees

Car lifted to hips

Car lifted to chest

III. What Did You Discover?

❶ How high did you need to lift the board or cardboard sheet before the car began to move?

_____

_____

❷ Why do you think the car on the ground did not move?

_____

_____

❸ Do you think that as you lifted the ramp higher and higher, the car gained more and more gravitational stored energy? Why or why not?

_____

_____

❹ Do you think there was more kinetic energy (moving energy) in the car as you lifted the ramp? Why or why not?

_____

_____

_____

❺ Was this result what you expected? Why or why not?

_____

_____

_____

PHYSICS

IV. Why?

In this experiment you took a toy car, and placing it on a board or cardboard sheet, you observed how the amount of gravitational stored energy changed as you lifted the board. In the first observation, you saw that the car did not move. When the car was not elevated and was sitting flat on the ground, the car did not have any gravitational stored energy. As you lifted the car to your ankles, the car was "given" gravitational stored energy by your body. The car may not have moved until you lifted the ramp to your knees or to your hips, but each time you lifted the car you "gave" it more gravitational stored energy until there was enough stored energy for the car to move down the ramp.

When the car moved down the ramp, the gravitational stored energy was converted to kinetic (or moving) energy. You may have observed that the higher you lifted the toy car, the faster the car moved down the ramp. Since the toy car has more gravitational stored energy as it is lifted higher, there is more energy to convert to kinetic energy. As a result, there is more kinetic energy as the car goes down the ramp.

PHYSICS

V. Just For Fun

How high do you have to lift the toy car to smash a marshmallow placed at the end of the ramp?

Put a few marshmallows at the end of your ramp. Raise the ramp, and let the toy car roll down. See if you can get the toy car to hit a marshmallow. How high do you have to lift the car for it to smash the marshmallow? Record your observations.

Height of Car	Did it smash the marshmallow?	
Car flat	YES	NO
Car lifted to ankles	YES	NO
Car lifted to knees	YES	NO
Car lifted to hips	YES	NO
Car lifted to chest	YES	NO

Hint: You may have to lift the ramp to your head or higher! Also, what would happen if you used a heavier car?

One way scientists make discoveries is by changing a part of their experiment to see what will happen. Try making other changes to this experiment. What would happen if you used a longer ramp? A shorter ramp? What other changes could you make? Try one or more of them and see what you discover.

Changes to the Experiment and Results of the Changes

Experiment 13

Playing With Physics

I. Observe It

❶ Take two marbles. Roll one marble into the other marble.

❷ Draw what happens to the two marbles.

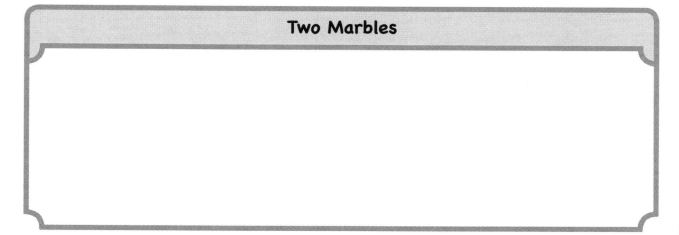

Two Marbles

❸ Take three playing cards and make a small card house.

❹ Roll a marble so it hits the card house. Draw what happens to the cards.

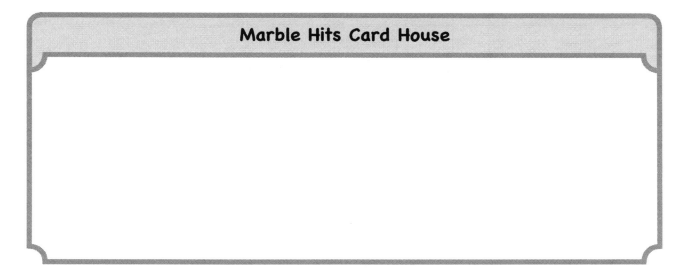

Marble Hits Card House

❺ Find a shallow jar top. A pickle jar top would work well. Fill it with vinegar.

❻ Add 15 milliliters (1 tablespoon) of baking soda to the vinegar.

❼ Draw what happens.

Vinegar and Baking Soda

PHYSICS

❽ Fill the shallow lid with vinegar again, and make a card house above the lid.

❾ Place 15 milliliters (1 tablespoon) of baking soda on top of the card house. Tip the card house with your finger so the baking soda falls into the vinegar. Record your observations below.

Card House Plus Baking Soda and Vinegar

PHYSICS

❿ Now assemble all the steps into a short series. Take one marble and place it a few inches from the card house. Place the shallow lid of vinegar under the card house, then place a tablespoon of baking soda on top of the card house. Roll a second marble into the marble that is close to the card house. Record your observations below.

Marble-->Marble-->Card House w/Baking Soda-->Vinegar

II. Think About It

❶ Think about the different types of energy you assembled in this short series.

❷ Review what you learned about energy in this chapter of the *Student Textbook*. Note how energy is neither created nor destroyed but simply converted from one form to another.

❸ In the table below list the type of energy you think the object started with and the type of energy you think it was converted to. Use the following energy descriptions:

Kinetic energy (rolling)
Kinetic energy (falling)
Stored energy (chemical)
Stored energy (gravitational)
Chemical energy

Object	Started With	Converted To
marble-->marble		
marble-->card house		
card house upright--> card house falling		
baking soda or vinegar -->baking soda + vinegar		

PHYSICS

III. What Did You Discover?

❶ What happened to the energy of one marble when you rolled it into another marble that was not moving?

_____

_____

❷ What happened to the energy of the marble when you rolled it and it hit the card house?

_____

_____

_____

❸ What happened to the energy in the baking soda (or the vinegar) when you added the two together?

_____

_____

_____

❹ What happened to the energy of the marble you rolled when you put all the steps together?

_____

_____

_____

❺ What do you think happened to all the energy at the end of your experiment? Where did it go?

_____

_____

_____

_____

PHYSICS

IV. Why?

In this experiment you explored how different forms of energy can be converted from one form to another. You rolled a marble and watched it use kinetic energy to move. You had that marble strike another marble, and you observed how the kinetic energy of the first marble was converted into kinetic energy in the second marble.

You also rolled a marble to hit a card house, converting the kinetic energy of the rolling marble into the kinetic energy of the falling cards. You observed how the gravitational stored energy of the top card was converted into kinetic energy when it fell.

When you put the vinegar underneath the card house and placed baking soda on top, you converted chemical stored energy into chemical energy when the baking soda and vinegar came together.

In each case, you observed energy being converted from one form into another. This is how energy works. You can't create energy, and you can't destroy it. You can only move it from one object to another or convert it from one form to another.

What do you think happened to all the energy at the end of your experiment? Where did it go?

PHYSICS

V. Just For Fun

Create your own series for converting energy from one form to another.

Here are some ideas—see if you can connect them.

- Rolling marbles

- Dominoes side by side

- Vinegar and baking soda

- Stacked blocks

- An electric car

- An electric train

- Marshmallow on one end of a tongue depressor, a steel ball or marble dropped on the other end

PHYSICS

Series Ideas

_____

_____

_____

_____

_____

_____

_____

_____

_____

_____

Draw your series setup.

Write or draw what happened.

PHYSICS

Experiment 14

Geology Every Day

Even before geology became a science, people observed rocks and landscapes, mountains, lakes, and rivers. In this experiment you will make observations about how geology affects your daily life.

I. Think About It

Think about where you live.

❶ Do you live in a city or in the country?

_____

❷ Is your house built with concrete, stone, brick, or some combination of these?

_____

❸ Where did the builders find the concrete, stone, or brick for your house?

_____

_____

_____

❹ Do you live near mountains or on the plains? Near a lake, the ocean, or in the desert? Describe what you think the area where you live is like.

_____

_____

_____

_____

GEOLOGY

❺ What is the weather like where you live? Do you have lots
   of rain, tornadoes, or hurricanes? Describe some kinds of
   weather that happen where you live.

   _____

   _____

   _____

   _____

   _____

❻ Do you live near a volcano? Are there earthquakes where you
   live? What do you think it is like to live in these areas?

   _____

   _____

   _____

   _____

❼ How much does the geology of where you live affect your
   life? In what ways is your life affected?

   _____

   _____

   _____

   _____

   _____

   _____

GEOLOGY

II. Observe It

❶ Make a list of all the geological features you see in a day, such as mountains, rivers, lakes, or an ocean.

_____

_____

_____

_____

_____

_____

_____

❷ Observe the weather where you live and write down what you experience—hot weather, cold weather, rain, fog, snow, drought, etc.

_____

_____

_____

_____

_____

_____

_____

GEOLOGY

❸ List the kinds of animals that live near you. Write down the names of any wildlife that you see, such as foxes, coyotes, squirrels, snakes, lizards, ants, bears, sparrows, or any other kind of wildlife.

_____

_____

_____

_____

_____

_____

_____

❹ List the types of plants that live near you. Write down the plants that grow around your home, such as green grass, flowers, cactus, or weeds.

_____

_____

_____

_____

_____

_____

_____

GEOLOGY

III. What Did You Discover?

❶ Do the mountains, rivers, oceans, or plains affect the kinds of wildlife you see? Why or why not?

_____

_____

_____

❷ Does the weather affect the mountains, rivers, or oceans? Why or why not?

_____

_____

_____

❸ Does the kind of soil you live near affect what kinds of plants can grow? Why or why not?

_____

_____

_____

❹ Does the area where you live affect the kind of house you live in? Why or why not?

_____

_____

_____

GEOLOGY

IV. Why?

If you live near a volcano, or if the place where you live experiences earthquakes, you might be very aware of the geology around you. However, it is easy to forget that geology affects our daily lives even without earthquakes and volcanoes. Where your house is located, the kind of plants and animals you see, the weather you experience, and the view from your house are all determined by geology.

V. Just For Fun

Imagine what it might be like to live on the Moon. What would the landscape look like—flat, mountainous, or...? Where would you want your house to be located? What would it be made of? Would you have any weather? Would you see animals and plants, and if so, what kinds?

On the next page, draw a picture of your home on the Moon. If you would like to write down some of your ideas first, you can use the lines below.

_____

_____

_____

_____

_____

_____

GEOLOGY

Home on the Moon

GEOLOGY

Experiment 15

Mud Pies

I. Observe It

❶ Go outside to your backyard, to a park, or any place where there is dirt that can be collected. Using a small shovel, dig a sample of the dirt and put it into a small pail or plastic container.

❷ Look through the dirt sample you collected. In the space below, draw what you observe.

GEOLOGY

❸ Using your hands, separate the dirt from any small or large rocks you collected in your sample.

❹ Notice that rocks are different from dirt. Explain, write, or draw how you can tell the difference between rocks and dirt.

_____

_____

_____

_____

_____

_____

GEOLOGY

❺ Take about .25 liter (1 cup) of the dirt mixture and put it in a tall, clear glass container. Pour water into the container so that it covers the dirt completely. Make sure that there is 5-8 centimeters (2-3 inches) of water above the dirt.

❻ Stir the dirt gently with your fingers. Watch what happens to the water that was above the dirt and observe what happens to the rocks. Write or draw your observations below.

_____

_____

_____

_____

_____

GEOLOGY

❼ Allow the mixture to settle. Observe what happens and write or draw your observations below.

_____

_____

_____

_____

_____

II. Think About It

❶ Can you tell the difference between rocks and soil (dirt)? If so, can you explain this difference?

_____

_____

_____

_____

_____

❷ When you added water to the soil, mixed it up, and allowed it settle, what did you observe?

_____

_____

_____

_____

_____

GEOLOGY

❸ Add 60 milliliters (1/4 cup) of flour to the mixture. Stir the mixture and allow it to settle. Observe what happens and write or draw your observations on the following page.

_____

_____

_____

_____

_____

_____

III. What Did You Discover?

❶ What are some of the differences you observed between rocks and dirt?

_____

_____

_____

❷ When you added water to the rock/dirt mixture, did the water get cloudy? If so, why do think that happened?

_____

_____

_____

❸ When you allowed the rock/dirt mixture to settle, did you observe layers forming? If so, why do you think this happened?

_____

_____

_____

❹ When you added the flour, did the flour form a layer as the mixture settled? Why or why not?

_____

_____

_____

GEOLOGY

IV. Why?

In this experiment you observed the differences between rocks and dirt and how both rocks and dirt behave in a water mixture. When you mixed the rocks and dirt with water, you got what is called a slurry. When this slurry was allowed to settle, you noticed that the rocks settled first, and the lighter dirt particles settled last. When the flour was added, you could probably see a layer of flour settling between layers of rocks and dirt.

In your textbook you learned about sedimentary rocks. In this experiment you observed how sedimentary rocks are formed when sediments (rocks, dirt, and other particles) settle. The heavier particles will settle first, and the lighter particles will settle last. This causes layers to be formed.

Sedimentary rocks are formed when these layers are put under great pressure. When you see a sedimentary rock, you can observe different layers in the rock. These rock layers are created in the same way you created layers with your rock, dirt, flour, and water mixture.

GEOLOGY

V. Just For Fun

You can make your own edible sedimentary rock. Try the recipe below. Observe how the layers settle.

Get a cake mix and follow the directions on the package to make a batter. Before pouring the batter into a baking pan, stir in some nuts, gumdrops, and chocolate chips or M&Ms.

When you cut the cooled cake, observe the layers that have formed. In the box below, draw the cake and its layers.

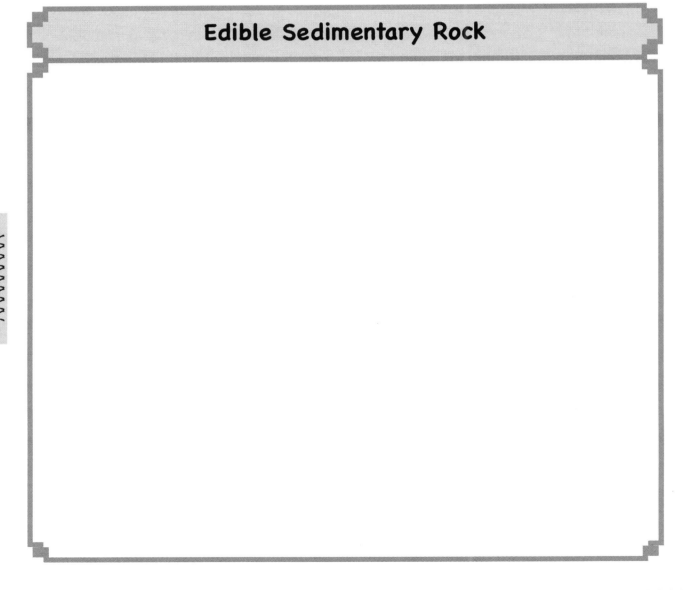

Edible Sedimentary Rock

GEOLOGY

Experiment 16

The Shape of Earth

I. Think About It

Why do you think the Earth is shaped like a slightly smashed ball that is a little farther across than it is from top to bottom? Write or draw your ideas below.

_____

_____

_____

_____

_____

_____

_____

GEOLOGY

II. Observe It

❶ Take a baseball and place it on the floor. Try to spin the ball in place.

❷ Write or draw your observations below.

_____

_____

_____

_____

_____

_____

GEOLOGY

❸ Fill a balloon with water, tie it closed, and place it on the floor.

❹ Without breaking the balloon, spin it in place. Write or draw your observations below.

_____

_____

_____

_____

_____

_____

_____

III. What Did You Discover?

❶ Did the baseball change shape when you spun it on the floor? Why or why not?

_____

_____

_____

❷ Did the water balloon change shape when you spun it on the floor? Why or why not?

_____

_____

_____

❸ Can you change the shape of the baseball with your hands? Why or why not?

_____

_____

_____

❹ Can you change the shape of the water balloon with your hands? Why or why not?

_____

_____

_____

GEOLOGY

IV. Why?

Since a baseball is solid all the way to its center, its shape cannot easily be changed. A water balloon has a soft center, which means that its shape can be more easily changed than can the shape of a baseball.

We live on the hard, rocky part of Earth (the crust), but Earth is mostly soft or fluid inside. The Earth spins around an axis, which is an imaginary straight line that goes through the center of the Earth. This spinning motion creates an outward-directed force called *centrifugal force*. Centrifugal force causes the Earth's center to bulge slightly as the soft part of the inner Earth is forced outward by centrifugal force.

In this experiment the balloon that holds the water is similar to the crust and outer mantle of the Earth. Both the balloon and the hard outer layers of Earth surround a soft center. As the balloon is spun, it is able to change in shape in response to centrifugal force. The crust and outer mantle and the soft part of the inner Earth have also changed in shape due to the centrifugal force caused by the spinning of the Earth. This has created the bulge at the equator of the Earth.

(See the *Astronomy* section for more about the effects of Earth's spin on its axis.)

GEOLOGY

V. Just For Fun

Sometimes a scientist will get an idea about what something is like or how it works. Then the scientist will do an experiment by thinking about that idea and all its possibilities. This is called a *thought experiment.*

Here is a thought experiment for you to try. Use your imagination while doing this thought experiment. Write or draw your ideas below and on the next page.

THOUGHT EXPERIMENT

We have discovered that the Earth has a slightly flattened ball shape. Think about what it might be like if, instead of being round, the Earth were shaped like a cube.

Do you think anything would be different if Earth were shaped like a cube? Would travel be different? What would happen when you came to an edge or a corner? What things can you think of that might be different?

Write or draw your ideas.

GEOLOGY

_____

_____

_____

_____

_____

_____

_____

_____

Thought Experiment
EARTH AS A CUBE

GEOLOGY

Experiment 17

Mud Volcanoes

In this experiment you will explore how the thickness of lava determines the type of mountain that can be formed by a volcano.

I. Think About It

❶ What happens when you pour thick syrup on your pancakes?

_____

_____

_____

❷ How fast does it flow from the pancakes to the plate?

_____

_____

_____

❸ What do you think would happen if you poured water on your pancakes?

_____

_____

_____

❹ How fast do you think the water would flow from the pancakes to the plate?

_____

_____

_____

GEOLOGY

❺ What happens when you mix dirt with a little bit of water?
Does it make a good mud pie? Why or why not?

_____

_____

_____

_____

_____

❻ What happens when you mix dirt with a lot of water? Does it
make a good mud pie? Why or why not?

_____

_____

_____

_____

_____

II. Observe It

Part I. Mix the following:

❶ Mix .5 liter (about 2 cups) of dirt with .25 liter (about 1 cup)
of water and label it "**A.**

❷ Mix .5 liter (about 2 cups) of dirt with .5 liter (about 2 cups)
of water and label it "**B**"

❸ Mix .5 liter (about 2 cups) of dirt with .75 liter (about 3 cups)
of water and label it "**C**"

Part II. Observe your three mixtures. In the chart below, write the answers to the following questions.

① Is the mixture thick or thin?

② Can you form a mud pie with the mixture? Why or why not?

③ Which is the thickest mixture?

④ Which is the thinnest mixture?

GEOLOGY

Question	A	B	C
①			
②			
③			
④			

Part III. Now take each mixture (**A**, **B**, and **C**) and pour a little of each on the ground. Pour each mixture in its own area and label each area **A**, **B**, or **C**.

Observe what happens. In the chart below, write the answers to the following questions.

① Is the mixture easy or difficult to pour?

② Does the mixture stay together or spread out? Why?

③ How far does each mixture spread?

Question	A	B	C
①			
②			
③			

GEOLOGY

Part IV. After you pour the mixtures, allow the three areas to dry out. Then add another layer to each area. Pour the same mixture over the same spot where you poured it the first time. Add more layers, letting each layer dry out before adding another.

Observe what happens. In the chart below, write the answers to the following questions.

① Does the mixture form layers?

② How high are 2, 3, or 4 layers of each mixture?

③ How wide are 2, 3, or 4 layers of each mixture?

④ How far does each mixture spread?

Question	A	B	C
①			
②			
③			
④			

GEOLOGY

III. What Did You Discover?

❶ Which was the thickest mixture?

_____

❷ Which was the thinnest mixture?

_____

❸ How easy was it to pour the thickest mixture? Why?

_____

_____

❹ How easy was it to pour the thinnest mixture? Why?

_____

_____

❺ Which of the 3 mixtures would make the best cone volcano? Why?

_____

_____

_____

❻ Which of the 3 mixtures would make the best shield volcano? Why?

_____

_____

_____

GEOLOGY

IV. Why?

Volcanic lava begins as magma in the mantle of the Earth. When the magma finds its way to the surface, it is called lava. Lava is an extremely hot mixture of melted rocks and minerals.

Some lava is thick like mixture **A**, and some lava is thin like mixture **C**. When thick lava comes out of a volcano, it can form a cone volcano with steep sides. Because the lava is thick, it won't flow very far from the center. When thin lava comes out of a volcano, it can form a shield volcano. Because the lava is thin, it can flow very far away from the center of the volcano.

V. Just For Fun

❶ Using thick mud, build a cone-shaped volcano.

❷ Before the mud dries, use a pencil to poke a hole down the center of the cone.

❸ Allow the mud to dry.

❹ When it is dry, pour 15 milliliters (1 tablespoon) of baking powder down the hole.

❺ Next, gently pour in 15 milliliters (1 tablespoon) of vinegar.

❻ Observe what happens and draw a picture of it on the following page.

GEOLOGY

MUD VOLCANO

Experiment 18

Observing the Stars

I. Think About It

❶ Think about how you travel from one place to another place.

❷ How do you travel? By road? By plane? By boat? Write or draw your thoughts below.

_____

_____

_____

_____

_____

_____

ASTRONOMY

❸ What tools do the driver, pilot, or captain use to navigate? Write or draw below.

_____

_____

_____

❹ Do you think you can use the stars to navigate? Why or why not?

_____

_____

_____

_____

II. Observe It

❶ On a clear night, go outside and observe the stars and the Moon.

❷ In the space below, write down or draw where you are, the time of night, and the direction you are facing.

_____

_____

_____

_____

_____

ASTRONOMY

❸ Draw the stars you observe. Notice bright stars, big stars, and colored stars. Locate the Moon and draw what it looks like. Note stars that are near the Moon and draw them.

NIGHT 1

ASTRONOMY

❹ For the next 5 days, go to the same location and face the same direction as on Night 1. Observe the stars and Moon at the same time each night. Draw what you see. Note if the location of the Moon or stars changes.

NIGHT 2

NIGHT 3

NIGHT 4

ASTRONOMY

NIGHT 5

ASTRONOMY

NIGHT 6

III. What Did You Discover?

❶ Did any of the stars stay in the same place each night? How do you know?

_____

_____

_____

❷ Did any of the stars change places over several nights? How do you know?

_____

_____

_____

❸ Did the Moon look the same each night? Why or why not?

_____

_____

_____

❹ Did the stars near the Moon stay in the same place each night? Why or why not?

_____

_____

_____

ASTRONOMY

IV. Why?

Astronomers study the stars, planets, Moon, and Sun. Even before astronomy became a science, ancient people used the stars for navigation when they traveled. They also used the stars to plan for changes in weather and even to predict when the Sun would not shine because of a solar eclipse.

For example, the North Star, called Polaris, is above the North Pole and stays in the same place night after night. Using the North Star, travelers can know in which direction they are going. This helps them navigate their journey from one place to another.

Using the stars for navigation takes time to learn because it requires many observations over many days and nights. However, once you know how to use the stars, you can navigate a journey at night without getting lost.

ASTRONOMY

V. Just For Fun

Ancient people observed that some stars look like they are in a group. Stars that appear to be in a group are called a *constellation*. The ancient people gave these constellations names like Orion the Hunter, The Little Dipper, and The Dragon.

On a clear, dark night, observe the stars and find some star groups. What does each of your star groups make you think of? A person? An animal? An imaginary creature? An object? Pick one or more of your constellations and give each a name. Draw the stars in the constellation and connect the stars with lines to show the shape of your constellation.

Constellation _____

Constellation _____

Experiment 19

Earth in Space

I. Observe It

❶ Cut out the continents on the following page.

❷ Glue or tape the continents onto a large basketball with North America, South America, and Greenland on one side and Australia, Africa, Europe, Russia, and Asia on the other side.

❸ Cut a 2.5 cm (one inch) wide piece from the end of a toilet paper tube. This will give you a nice ring to place the basketball on. When you place the basketball on this cardboard ring, tilt the ball slightly off-center.

❹ Turn off the room lights. Walk several feet away from the basketball and shine light from a flashlight on the basketball.

❺ Leaving the flashlight shining on the basketball, rotate the basketball counterclockwise. Record your observations below.

_____

_____

_____

_____

_____

_____

_____

_____

_____

ASTRONOMY

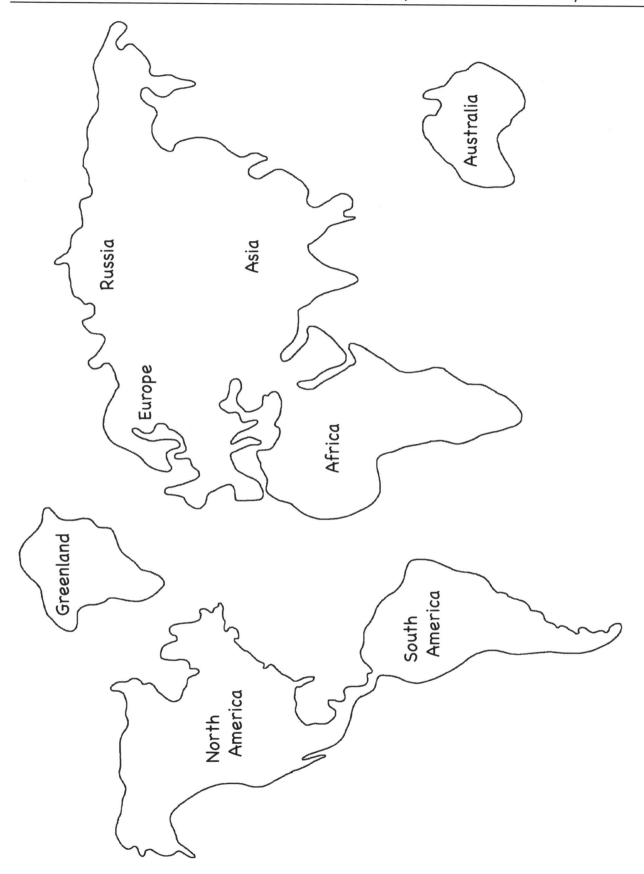

ASTRONOMY

❻ Hold a ping-pong ball a short distance away from the basketball. Move the ping-pong ball in a counterclockwise circle around the basketball. Record your observations below.

_____

_____

_____

_____

_____

_____

II. Think About It

❶ Can you determine how day and night are created by the rotation of Earth?

_____

_____

_____

_____

❷ Can you observe how a lunar eclipse forms (where Earth casts a shadow on the Moon)?

_____

_____

_____

_____

❸ Can you observe how a solar eclipse forms (where the Moon casts a shadow on Earth)?

_____

_____

_____

_____

ASTRONOMY

❹ Using the basketball and flashlight, can you show how the seasons are created? Explain how you would do this.

_____

_____

_____

_____

_____

III. What Did You Discover?

❶ Explain how day and night occur.

_____

_____

_____

_____

❷ Explain how a lunar eclipse occurs.

_____

_____

_____

❸ Explain how a solar eclipse occurs.

_____

_____

_____

❹ What causes the different seasons?

_____

_____

_____

ASTRONOMY

IV. Why?

In this experiment you observed what happens when the Sun shines on the Earth and the Moon. In this experiment the Sun is represented by the flashlight, Earth is represented by the basketball, and the Moon is represented by the ping-pong ball.

When you rotated the basketball (Earth), the flashlight (Sun) was shining on different parts of the ball. This action, (the Sun shining on a rotating Earth) is what causes night and day.

When you took the ping-pong ball (Moon) and rotated it around the basketball (Earth), you observed how the Moon casts a shadow on Earth when the Moon is between the Sun and the Earth. This illustrates a solar eclipse. You also observed how the Earth casts a shadow on the Moon when the Earth is between the Sun and the Moon. This arrangement illustrates a lunar eclipse.

You also found out how seasons occur. The Earth's tilt causes the seasons. As the Earth circles the Sun, some parts of Earth are tilted toward the Sun, receiving more heat energy, and some parts are tilted away, receiving less heat energy. This tilting of the Earth creates seasons as different parts of Earth are tilted toward or away from the Sun.

ASTRONOMY

V. Just For Fun

☼ Think about what it would be like if the Earth's axis still had the same tilt but the axis went through the equator instead of going through the North and South Poles. Would this change the seasons? Would it change night and day?

Try using the basketball and the flashlight to experiment with this idea.

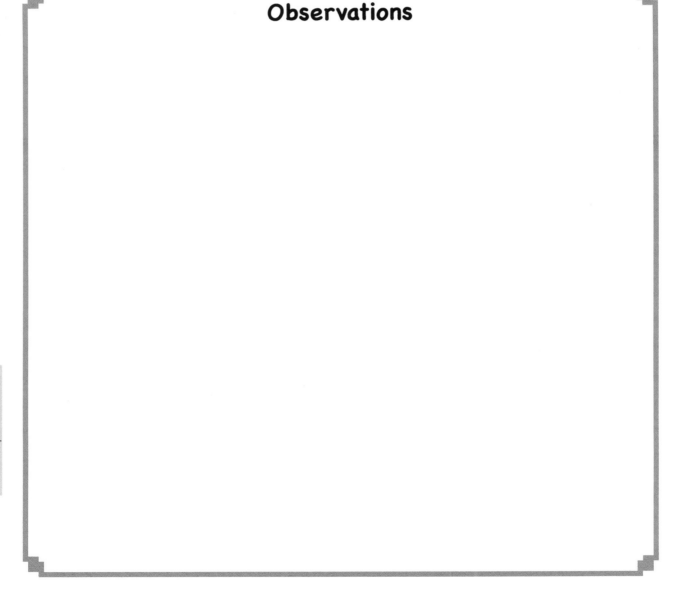

Observations

☼ Next, think about what would be different if the Earth's axis still went through the North and South Poles but was pointed directly at the Sun. Would this change the seasons where you live? Would it change night and day?

Try using the basketball and the flashlight to experiment with this idea.

Observations

ASTRONOMY

Experiment 20

Seeing the Moon

I. Observe It

❶ For fourteen days, observe the Moon at night. Notice any details about how it appears to you.

❷ Record your observations. Note the color and shape.

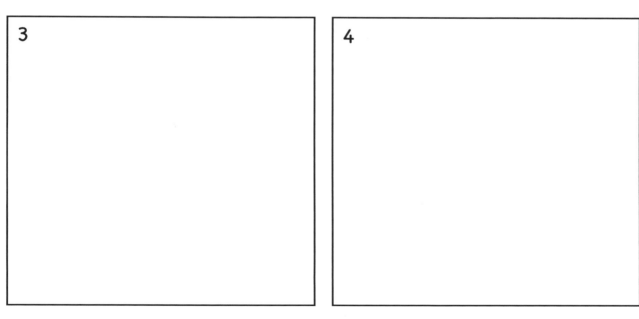

5

6

7

8

9

10

11

12

13

14

II. Think About It

❶ Does the color of the Moon stay the same or does it change?

_____

_____

_____

_____

❷ Does the shape of the Moon stay the same or does it change?

_____

_____

_____

_____

❸ What do you find most interesting about the Moon?

_____

_____

_____

_____

_____

_____

_____

ASTRONOMY

III. What Did You Discover?

❶ Why does the shape of the Moon change?

_____

_____

_____

_____

_____

❷ Where does the Moon get its light?

_____

_____

_____

_____

_____

❸ Do you think the Moon actually changes shape, or does it just look like it has changed shape because the Sun shines on different parts of the Moon on different days?

_____

_____

_____

_____

ASTRONOMY

IV. Why?

In this experiment you observed the shape and color of the Moon for several days. As the Moon circles the Earth, the shape of the Moon appears to change. Depending on when you began observing the Moon, you may have seen a full Moon (completely round), a half Moon (half-round), or a crescent Moon (a curved shape). Or you may not have been able to see the Moon at all.

As the Moon circles the Earth, the Sun illuminates different sections of the part of the Moon that faces us. This makes the shape of the Moon appear to change as we view it from Earth.

Since it takes almost one month for the Moon to circle the Earth, the Moon will cycle through the different shapes each month. The Moon will go from full Moon, to half Moon, to new (dark) Moon, back to half Moon, and then the cycle will begin again.

V. Just For Fun

In the evening find the Moon in the sky and draw what you see. Do you see details on the Moon? Is it a full Moon? Is it a half Moon? Does it look like there's a face on the Moon? Color the Moon as you see it and as you imagine it. Include any details you observe.

THE MOON

ASTRONOMY

Experiment 21

Modeling the Planets

I. Observe It

❶ In this experiment you will explore building models of the planets. Building models is important because it gives scientists a way to help them think about things that they cannot observe close up.

❷ Look at the illustrations of the planets in the *Student Textbook*. Note the sizes and colors of the eight planets. Make notes about what you observe.

_____

_____

_____

_____

_____

_____

_____

_____

_____

_____

❸ Take the eight Styrofoam balls and assign a Styrofoam ball to represent each planet.

❹ Using the information you've collected, paint each Styrofoam ball to look like the planet it represents.

ASTRONOMY

II. Think About It

❶ How did you decide which Styrofoam ball to assign to Jupiter?

_____

_____

_____

❷ How did you decide which Styrofoam ball to assign to Mercury?

_____

_____

_____

❸ What similarities and differences did you notice between the planets?

_____

_____

_____

_____

_____

_____

_____

_____

ASTRONOMY

III. What Did You Discover?

❶ What did building models of the planets help you observe?

_____

_____

_____

_____

❷ What features did you notice that make the planets different from each other? How did you use these features so each planet could be identified from your model of it?

_____

_____

_____

_____

_____

_____

❸ How easy or difficult was it to model the planets?

_____

_____

_____

_____

_____

ASTRONOMY

IV. Why?

In this experiment you explored building models to help you understand more about Earth and the other seven planets that orbit the Sun. Since scientists are not able to go to each of the planets, they use tools to make observations. Then, based on their observations, the scientists make models that show what they think the planets are like.

Models may not be accurate, but they are a scientist's best guess based on the information available. Sometimes using a model will lead a scientist to ask more questions. The answers may add to the scientist's knowledge and can result in changes to the model that make it more accurate.

Scientists can also make mental models of ideas that they have about how things work or why things are the way they are. These mental models may be written in words or pictures or explained with mathematics, and they can lead to many new discoveries.

ASTRONOMY

V. Just For Fun

Think of some other things you could use to build models of the planets. Maybe you could find fruits of different sizes to be the planets. Are there vegetables that would work? Candies? Could you use a mixture of different kinds of items? See if you can invent some different ways to model the planets.

Ideas for Making Planet Models

_____

_____

_____

_____

_____

_____

_____

_____

_____

_____

_____

_____

_____

ASTRONOMY

Planet Model Drawing

Experiment 22

Putting It All Together

I. Think About It

❶ How is chemistry connected to biology?

_____

_____

_____

_____

_____

❷ How is biology connected to physics?

_____

_____

_____

_____

❸ How is physics connected to astronomy?

_____

_____

_____

_____

_____

❹ How is astronomy connected to geology?

_____

_____

_____

_____

_____

❺ How is geology connected to chemistry?

_____

_____

_____

_____

_____

❻ How do chemistry, biology, physics, geology, and astronomy all connect to each other?

_____

_____

_____

_____

_____

_____

_____

II. Observe It

❶ Observe a living thing, for example, a ladybug.

❷ Answer the following questions, and write down what kinds of science would help you to arrive at each answer: chemistry, biology, physics, geology, astronomy.

• What do _____ eat?

_____

_____

• How do _____ digest food?

_____

_____

• How do _____ move?

_____

_____

• Where do _____ live?

_____

_____

• How long do _____ live?

_____

_____

- How big are _____?

  _____

  _____

- How much does a _____ weigh?

  _____

  _____

- What do _____ breathe?

  _____

  _____

- Would _____ be found on the Moon?
  Why or why not?

  _____

  _____

- What are some other questions you have about
  _____ and which kinds of science would
  answer those questions?

  _____

  _____

  _____

  _____

  _____

III. What Did You Discover?

❶ Does it help to know chemistry to find out how a
_____ digests food? Why or why not?

_____

_____

_____

❷ Does it help to know astronomy to find out if a
_____ can live on the Moon? Why or why not?

_____

_____

_____

❸ Does it help to know physics to find out how a
_____ moves? Why or why not?

_____

_____

_____

❹ Does it help to know geology to find out where a
_____ lives? Why or why not?

_____

_____

_____

IV. Why?

Science is really a mixture of five core science subjects: chemistry, physics, biology, geology, and astronomy.

Even though scientists specialize in a particular area of study, it is important for scientists to know about other scientific subjects. Knowing about ladybugs and other living things requires learning about not just biology, but also chemistry, physics, geology, and astronomy.

V. Just For Fun

Think of a living thing or an object you are interested in. Write down the name of the thing.

Using the chart on the next page, write down everything you know about that living thing or object, and ask yourself whether what is known is related to chemistry, physics, biology, geology, or astronomy.

Thing: _____

FACT	SCIENCE SUBJECT

More REAL SCIENCE-4-KIDS Books
by Rebecca W. Keller, PhD

Focus Series (unit study program — each title has a Student Textbook with accompanying Laboratory Workbook, Teacher's Manual, Study Folder, Quizzes, and Recorded Lectures)

Focus On Elementary Chemistry
Focus On Elementary Biology
Focus On Elementary Physics
Focus On Elementary Geology
Focus On Elementary Astronomy

Focus On Middle School Chemistry
Focus On Middle School Biology
Focus On Middle School Physics
Focus On Middle School Geology
Focus On Middle School Astronomy

Focus On High School Chemistry

Building Blocks Series (year-long study program — each Student Textbook has accompanying Laboratory Notebook, Teacher's Manual, Lesson Plan, and Quizzes)

Exploring the Building Blocks of Science Book K (Coloring Book)
Exploring the Building Blocks of Science Book 1
Exploring the Building Blocks of Science Book 2
Exploring the Building Blocks of Science Book 3
Exploring the Building Blocks of Science Book 4
Exploring the Building Blocks of Science Book 5
Exploring the Building Blocks of Science Book 6
Exploring the Building Blocks of Science Book 7
Exploring the Building Blocks of Science Book 8

Super Simple Science Experiments Series

21 Super Simple Chemistry Experiments
21 Super Simple Biology Experiments
21 Super Simple Physics Experiments
21 Super Simple Geology Experiments
21 Super Simple Astronomy Experiments

Kogs-4-Kids Series (interdisciplinary workbooks that connect science to other areas of study)

Physics Connects to Language
Biology Connects to Language
Chemistry Connects to Language
Geology Connects to Language
Astronomy Connects to Language

Note: A few titles may still be in production.

Gravitas Publications Inc.
www.realscience4kids.com

GRAVITAS
PUBLICATIONS